LifeCaps Presents:

American Trapper:

The Life and Death of American

Frontiersman Hugh Glass

By Fergus Mason

BookCaps™ Study Guides

Cover Image © Natika - Fotolia

D0683549

Table of Contents

About LifeCaps

LifeCaps is an imprint of BookCaps™ Study Guides. With each book, a lesser known or sometimes forgotten life is recapped. We publish a wide array of topics (from baseball and music to literature and philosophy), so check our growing catalogue regularly (www.bookcaps.com) to see our newest books.

Introduction

He woke to a world of pain and darkness.

Was he even awake? At first he didn't know. He could barely remember the last time he'd been conscious, it had been so long, and what he was experiencing now emerged seamlessly from the red nightmare of fever dreams. The dark phantoms that had hunted him through those dreams slowly faded, submerged in the rising tide of pain. At first, as his mind struggled up from the depths, the pain overwhelmed the power of thought and he just lay there, soaking it up.

Then gradually, circuits in his brain fought clear of agony's vise and started to communicate. It was dark, but muffled noises told him it was daylight. He didn't remember what those chirps and rustles were for now – that would come, he thought – but he knew they'd once been familiar to him and they meant the sun was up. So why was it dark? He tried to move an arm and the pain rose again, washing all thoughts away in a flare of blazing sensation.

Then it subsided once more and he could think again. Where did it hurt? Slowly, the mental equipment rusty from days of disuse, he started to take inventory. His head hurt foully. The muscles in his shoulders and arms ached, and bright lines of hurt told him he had been grievously slashed. His chest and back were in no better shape. His legs were perhaps the worst. The pain there had a different quality. One of them didn't feel whole; broken for sure, he realized. And that wasn't the worst of it. Everywhere else on his body the pain was sharp, clean and deep. In the broken leg it was a hot, rotten pulse. He had an infection, and infection meant death. Once a wound started to redden and throb there was no treatment, just a gradual swelling and putrefaction until the poison in the blood reached his heart and killed him.

But he didn't want to die here.

Why did he not want to die? At first he wasn't sure. This pain was unbearable; it would be simpler, more pleasant, just to sink back into the red dreams and wait for the end. But he couldn't. There was something else he had to do, and he had to stay alive to do it.

After some minutes he tried moving his arm again. It hurt, but if he moved slowly it could be done. Twigs and dry leaves crackled, but something heavier was pressing down on him too. He groped in the dark around his head. Finally, his questing hand reached the edge of something and he forced the fingers painfully closed. Inch by inch he dragged the burning arm down towards his chest, and a faint gray light reached his eyes. It hurt them. Well, why not? Everything else hurt, so why not his eyes?

The heavy thing that covered him was an enormous thick pelt, draped over his battered body. As it slipped away from his face the twigs and leaves that had been heaped on top of it cascaded onto him. He barely noticed, obsessed with slowly dragging the pelt away. Finally his upper body was free. As his eyes adjusted to the light he looked around, moving his head slowly. He lay in a shallow pit. Something stirred in his tormented mind. Dead people lay in pits, but not like this one. He'd seen that – hell, he'd helped dig more than a few himself. Those were deep pits, hacked from the earth with tools. This was just a gentle depression scraped out between two trees. Had someone tried to bury him?

He tried to stand, to get out of the makeshift grave, but sagged back weakly. His legs couldn't take his weight. In fact they could barely move. Slowly, gritting his teeth against the agony it provoked, he rolled over onto his stomach. Then he reached out, sank his fingers into the soil and began dragging himself, inch by inch, from the pit.

It took him nearly an hour, but finally he was back above ground, sitting with his back to a tree and looking out at the infinite wilderness that surrounded him. Bit by bit memories returned to him. He remembered a titanic battle with some huge creature; that would explain his injuries. Then others like him, men, standing around his bleeding body discussing his fate. They'd decided to leave him, he recalled, because he was dying, and two had volunteered to stay with him and give him a decent burial.

But he wasn't dead, and they'd left him in a pit.

Now, buried deep at first in the pain that flamed through him, a new fire began to burn. Anger. He knew this wilderness; it was his home. He had the skills and tools needed to survive here, but those tools were gone – taken by the men left to care for him. All he had left was his knowledge and the building anger. That was why he couldn't die, he realized; that was what he had to do. He had to get his revenge. But the anger was trapped in this broken, infected carcass. How could he get the vengeance he craved if he was fated to die here?

That didn't matter, he decided, because he wasn't going to die. He had a name now, dredged up from among the raging flames of torment and fury. He didn't have much left, but he had a name. He was Hugh Glass, and he wasn't going to die.

Chapter 1

When the USA won its independence from Britain it was a lot smaller than it is today. The original Thirteen Colonies had steadily expanded to the west, but by 1800 they'd run up against Spanish territories that stretched from Louisiana in the south to the Canadian border and beyond. The states to the east of the Mississippi could have grown into a powerful and wealthy nation, but it could never have attained the position the USA holds today – and in fact might not have survived to the middle of the 19th century. The problem was solved by the Louisiana Purchase, a controversial move at the time but one that turned out to be the greatest of Thomas Jefferson's many contributions to the growth of the United States. For an astonishingly low price the Purchase secured the vital lower reaches of the Mississippi, eliminated the risk of Britain overrunning the French territory and surrounding the USA, and doubled the size of the country virtually overnight.

But such a huge and sudden expansion brought as many problems as it solved. The eastern states, outside a few major cities, were much more sparsely populated than they are today. Farmers were hacking new fields out of the ancient forests and industry was growing around the ports and rivers, while American ships and schooners were building an impressive whaling and fishing industry, but there weren't a lot of people available to expand into the new lands. Without American settlers there was a real risk they might drift back into the orbit of France, Spain or even Britain. The trouble was, the Purchase territory was a mystery to most Americans. Even the French and Spanish didn't really know much about it, and between them they'd owned it for two centuries. Most people were reluctant to abandon the places they knew and strike out into a foreboding wilderness. It was a place of vast forests, high mountains and savage animals. Violent rivers and an often harsh climate were a constant threat, and many of the native people were hostile to encroaching settlers. If the developing USA was ever to colonize and use this land it had to be explored, then tamed. In 1804 Jefferson sent Meriwether Lewis and William Clark on an expedition to cross the new land, and over the next two years they and their band of US Army volunteers marched right across the continent from St. Louis to the Pacific, then back again. It was an incredible achievement and helped develop new routes between the oceans but the expedition only covered a tiny percentage of the country's new interior.

To fully explore it, and begin the long process of turning it into the states that exist today, would be the work of a breed of hardy pioneers who were more at home in the wilderness than in the thriving towns of the East Coast. They were the Mountain Men – adventurers, trappers and hunters. Often wild or eccentric, they blazed a path west that helped make the USA a superpower. Many of their acts are controversial looking back from today's viewpoint, but they were heroes of their time. Hugh Glass was something more. Even the other Mountain men thought he was a hero.

Chapter 2

For a man who was later to develop such an awesome reputation among the toughest adventurers of his time, surprisingly little is known about Hugh Glass's origins and early life. In fact, trying to find out anything at all can be a real struggle. Many tales can be found to explain where he came from but most of them are based on legend, not fact. However some research can point us in the right direction.

One of the most credible stories is that Glass was born to an Irish immigrant family sometime around 1783, and probably in Pennsylvania. That's believable for several reasons. Firstly, the family name Glass originates in western Scotland, in the old Celtic kingdom of Dalriada, and through most of known British history there were frequent migrations between that region and Ireland. Glass and its many variants are still common names in Ireland today, so an Irish-American background seems likely. The date also fits in with what's known about his later life. When his best-known exploits occurred he was a mature man with years of experience in the wilderness, but still young enough to be physically fit and tough. As for his being born in Pennsylvania, that state produced many explorers and hunters, and was also famous for manufacturing high quality rifles.

Many men from Pennsylvania left the state to seek their fortune elsewhere, and it seems likely that the young Hugh was one of them. Neighboring New York and the New England states were growing centers of trade and fishing, and surviving accounts strongly suggest that he went to sea. There, according to the best information we have, he faced all the dangers of early 19th century seafaring – storms, harsh living conditions and brutally hard, risky work in the complicated rigging of a sailing ship. And there was one more, usually associated with the Caribbean in the previous century but still a real hazard all up the Atlantic coast until well into the 19th century: piracy.

Jean Lafitte was born, probably in northwest France, sometime around 1780. It's believed he went to sea young, on a ship owned by his trader father, but by 1803 he was in New Orleans. The Louisiana Purchase opened up trade the length of the Mississippi and through the Gulf of Mexico, and many US shipowners began sailing from there after 1803, but it was also a popular port with ships from other nations. Within a few years of his arrival Lafitte and his brother had built up a steady smuggling business and by 1810, from their port on Louisiana's Barataria Bay, they had drifted into piracy. Not long after that Lafitte captured the ship Hugh Glass had signed on with and Hugh, by now in his late 20s, was persuaded to join the pirate's crew.

Lafitte wasn't a flamboyant sociopath like Blackbeard Teach or a rum-soaked adventurer like Calico Jack Rackham; he was a businessman, and ran an elaborate scheme that involved picking up legitimate cargoes in New Orleans and doctoring the manifests to allow him to sell smuggled or pirated goods. However he was still a pirate, and life on one of his ships would have been even harsher than on a merchantman. Hugh seems to have spent at least a year as a sea robber, but perhaps that was enough to persuade him to stay on land from then on. By the time he next appears firmly in history he was already a seasoned backwoodsman.

Where did Hugh pick up the skills he had learned by the early 1820s? It's likely he returned to the northeast USA and found work with one of the fur companies that were growing rapidly at the time. In the 19th century a lot of clothing was made from fur, especially in regions where it got cold – and that included a lot of the USA. Winter hats were often made of cured pelts, and the warmest boots had a fur lining. Fur coats were a lot more common than they are now, and a lot more socially acceptable; they were worn for warmth, not as a fashion statement. Even more formal clothing might rely on the fur trappers, because many hats were made from felted beaver hair. Beavers, and many other animals, were being hunted and trapped in increasing numbers as explorers ventured into the Purchase lands, and the fur companies always had a vacancy for a hardy man who was willing to head out there and take his chances in the wilds. Almost certainly Hugh was one of them, because sometime between Jean Lafitte taking up piracy in 1810 and Hugh joining an expedition in 1822 he had become one of the Mountain Men.

It's likely Hugh had already made expeditions to Kansas or elsewhere on the Great Plains, because he's believed to have been made an honorary member of the Pawnee Nation.[i] Early explorers, especially those who traveled alone or in small groups, often had good relations with Native American tribes and even hunted together with them sometimes. These exchanges could benefit both sides. A wise trapper would carry a small stock of manufactured goods prized by the tribes – whiskey was the most notorious but others, such as steel axes and knives, were highly sought after and genuinely useful. In exchange they could gain knowledge about the land they moved through, where to find game and places to avoid. As long as the intruding white men were respectful and came in small numbers the indigenous people were usually friendly enough, although earlier experiences along the east coast had made many of them wary. Of course they had plenty to be wary about. The explorers and hunters would soon be followed by thousands, then millions, of settlers. As the American pioneers began to push west in greater numbers more of the tribes became hostile. That meant the newcomers traveled in larger groups for safety, which worried the natives even more. By the early 1820s hostile tribesmen were a major hazard to anyone heading west of the Mississippi, and a chain of events was underway that would eventually lead to open warfare. Hugh Glass was about to sign up for one of that war's first skirmishes.

Chapter 3

William Henry Ashley was a native of the Virginia Colony, but not long after the Louisiana Purchase he moved to St. Louis, a former French city in what was then the Missouri Territory. During the War of 1812 he became a Brigadier General in the Missouri Militia, and after the war he continued with his previous business ventures, including a gunpowder factory. When Missouri became the 24th state of the Union in 1821 he was the first Lieutenant Governor. Still, he was curious about what wealth might lie further west, and after all Missouri is known as the gateway to the west. In 1822 he decided to find out.

Teaming up with another former militia officer, bullet maker Andrew Henry, Ashley started investigating the fur trade up the Missouri River. Then in July 1822 a new law was passed that made it illegal to sell alcohol to natives. St. Louis fur traders had been collecting materials by hiring Indian hunters to trap or shoot animals and bring them the pelts, and they were often paid in liquor. Even when they weren't, large amounts of alcohol were often involved, making it easier for unscrupulous traders to cheat them. The new legislature was concerned at the criminality resulting from this and cracked down just a year after statehood, but already whiskey was so firmly embedded in the business that it became impossible to hire hunters without it. Faced with collapse, the fur trade looked for a new supply. Ashley decided that was an opening he could fill, and together with Major Henry he founded the Rocky Mountain Fur Company.

The fur business was already thriving and the leaders were the Hudson's Bay Company, the North West Company and the American Fur Company (which played a major part in founding the Astor fortune). The industry's center of gravity was to the north, in British-controlled Canada, but there was a lot of potential further south and the plan was fundamentally sound. Instead of relying on Indians a series of temporary camps could be set up along the upper reaches of the Missouri, where trappers could collect on arranged dates to deliver the furs they'd collected. To initiate the scheme Ashley and Henry planned to set off with a large party, and in late 1822 they began advertising in St. Louis newspapers for "One Hundred enterprising young men to ascend the river Missouri to its source, there to be employed for one, two, or three years."

The prospect of a long trip into unexplored territory for years of hard, dangerous work would send the average person running, but to the Mountain Men it was an irresistible challenge. Scores of pioneers flocked in to join the expedition and they included some of the most important figures in the conquest of the American West. Kit Carson, the Indian fighter, was one of them. David Edward Jackson helped open the Oregon Trail to the Pacific southwest. Freed slave James Beckwourth went on to find a pass through the Sierra Nevadas that opened the way to California and still bears his name. Jedediah Smith, another volunteer, had been the first European to travel overland to the Salt Lake and then to California. It was a distinguished list of explorers and adventurers, and Hugh Glass was on it too.

Was it just the prospect of money that encouraged him to sign on? It's impossible to know. That was certainly what motivated most of his companions. They wanted to strike out west and build new lives for themselves in the – to them – promising country out towards their nation's new frontiers. In general they were young men, few out of their twenties and some still in their teens. Hugh was older though – almost forty. He was also more educated, a fact we can tell from his one surviving letter. Most Mountain Men couldn't write beyond a scrawl, but the expressive prose of Hugh Glass points to a literate and thoughtful man. Maybe he just preferred the solitude of the wild country, or the challenge of exploring somewhere new; either way, he was about to get it.

Chapter 4

The expedition, which had become known as "Ashley's Hundred", set out from St. Louis in early 1823. The plan was to travel by river as far as possible, so they began the journey in a small fleet of longboats. These were sturdy but sleek rowing boats, probably around thirty feet long and each large enough to carry ten men and all their supplies. Normally they would be rowed by pairs of men, sitting two to a bench and each working an oar on opposite sides of the boat, but when the wind was right a mast could be raised and a simple but effective lugsail hoisted. Their slim lines made them fast and agile, and they were – just – light enough for their crews to carry them past rapids or waterfalls if necessary. The first short leg of the trip took them up the Mississippi, then they turned into the Missouri River itself. The plan was to head to Grand River in South Dakota, then on to Yellowstone.

It was a hard journey. Traveling by river was much quicker than blazing a trail through the wilderness, but it was still hard work. The longboats were heavy craft, loaded down with supplies, and pulling the long sweep oars took a lot of effort. The diet was monotonous. They took bacon with them, and bags of salt, but the bulk of their rations was flour. For fresh meat they hunted, often eating the animals they killed for pelts. Game meat is lean and mountain men soon found their bodies craving fat, so beaver tail became a popular addition to their diet. To avoid scurvy they foraged berries, which are rich sources of vitamin C. Even so they often suffered boils in the winter. As they learned about new food sources from the Indians their diet improved, and their natural ingenuity also helped. It wasn't uncommon for each man to eat more than six pounds of meat each day, and fish were caught and fried by the hundred. With the constant physical effort they stayed lean and tough, and the Missouri River proved to be a rich source of fur. It was looking like a successful expedition, but a dangerous one.

On their hunting trips away from the river the men were moving through the territory of mountain lions, wolves and bears, but the biggest threat to them was the native people. Some of the tribes were friendly. Others were not, and the most implacably hostile were the Arikara people.

Also known as the Ree, the Arikara were an offshoot of the Pawnee people who had developed a separate identity sometime in the 15th century. They had adopted a semi-nomadic lifestyle around what's now South Dakota, planting and tending cornfields for part of the year then following the migrating bison herds to hunt. During the farming season they also grew beans, squash and tobacco. As well as supplying their own needs this gave them influence through trade, especially with the aggressive Sioux. The Sioux weren't farmers and had more of a tendency to war, but they also relied on the food the Arikara supplied and that gave the farmers leverage.

In the mid-18th century the Arikara Nation, located between the Grand and Cannonball rivers, had a population of up to 30,000 people; they controlled the Missouri River for a stretch of a hundred miles.[ii] Settled within a defined area even if they moved seasonally, they were a stable and prosperous people with no great interest in raiding or fighting. Then in the 1780s disease came. A series of smallpox epidemics devastated the tribe, reducing their numbers by up to three-quarters. The tribe worked out that it was the arrival of colonists that had caused the plague and it made them wary, but they were still friendly to Lewis and Clark in 1804. That expedition spent five days at an Arikara village and found them peaceful. Twenty years later things had changed radically.

Faced with increasing numbers of explorers and trappers the Arikara started to regard outsiders first with suspicion, then anger. Once they had been willing to trade crops for manufactured goods. Now they were more likely to attack any party they thought they could overwhelm. It's easy to understand this hostility. A way of life the tribe had followed for centuries was under immense pressure from the newcomers, who could use their firearms to wipe out bison herds that would have supported the Arikara indefinitely. Strange new diseases they had no immunity to might exterminate villages and extended families. Worst of all, the white men acted like they had a right to take whatever they wanted – land, game or resources. Lewis and Clark had persuaded the tribe to send an ambassador to President Jefferson, to discuss trade between them and the USA, but now the USA was steadily encroaching on their land. When they could they fought back - and as Lewis and Clark had noted, many of Arikara men now carried guns.[iii]

Ashley's Hundred soon found that the Arikara weren't happy with their presence. Their first encounter with a large group of Indians ended in disaster when they saw a village beside the river and, thinking they were friendly Pawnees, beached the boats to trade with them. The village wasn't Pawnee; its inhabitants were Arikara, and seeing a large group coming ashore they attacked. Two members of the party were killed and the rest returned to the boats and fled upriver, pursued by arrows and gunshots. Worse was to come, though.

On June 2 a large group of Arikara ambushed them. Caught at a narrow spot on the river, they were flayed with arrows and musket balls. Fifteen men died despite a desperate defense. Others were injured; Hugh Glass was one of them, taking a musket ball in the thigh that almost broke his femur. The ferocity of the attack forced them off the river and they continued, on foot, up the valley of the Grand River. They took their wounded and dying men with them. Glass, perhaps stiffened by experience of boarding a ship along with a horde of yelling pirates, had impressed his companions with his steadiness under fire. Now he demonstrated patience and compassion, tending the young Virginian John Gardner as he slowly succumbed to his injuries. Just before Gardner died he asked Hugh to send a final message back to his family. This he did, in a letter sent back for postage with a consignment of furs. While the note used abbreviations that modern writers don't – "yr" for "your", and "wh" for "which" – it's a long way from the barely literate scrawl of a man who'd picked up his letters in visits to frontier trading posts. Somewhere in Hugh Glass's past someone had sat him down and taught him both handwriting and grammar.

Shortly after the lethal attack they met a US Army patrol and reported it to them, but many of the group thought the military response – little more than a stern warning to the attackers' village – was feeble. In reprisal, two of the trappers returned to the village and set part of it on fire.[iv] Still, they were concerned. The Arikara were becoming ever more aggressive, and instead of showing the obedience the trappers thought they should they continued to attack any small group they found. If this continued, Major Henry worried, the defiance might spread to other tribes that so far had been friendly. With the whole native population against them they might have real trouble getting out of there alive.

Through June and July the expedition, having licked its wounds, continued exploring and trapping. Unlike Lewis and Clark they weren't striking boldly out across the continent, but meandering just beyond the borders of colonized territory. The Army had a small presence there, although it was already clear that wasn't doing much for their security, but if they needed to they could withdraw back to safety. With nearly a fifth of the party dead and several others injured by bullets or blades that must have been tempting for many. They were tough men, though, and the prospect of wealth pushed them on. July passed, then half of August. Now they were heading for Fort Henry, an outpost on the Yellowstone built by Major Henry the previous year. By August 23 they were close to the fork of the Yellowstone and Missouri, in what's now Perkins County, South Dakota. This was probably the most vulnerable part of the expedition. Fort Henry still lay hundreds of miles' march ahead of them. The safety of St. Louis was hundreds of miles behind.

Chapter 5

Hugh Glass didn't always work well as part of a group. Maybe that's why he abandoned the sea to become a Mountain Man; life on a sailing ship was cramped, with a complete lack of privacy and a constant need to work as part of a close-knit team. Out here in the Midwestern wilderness he had a lot more freedom. Even the loose-knit organization of the expedition chafed on him sometimes and he liked to get away on his own, either hunting or foraging for fruit and berries. He didn't go far from the main party on these excursions – if he shot a large animal he'd need help to get the carcass back – but he didn't really need to. Just a hundred yards into the woods he could find all the privacy he could ever want. The trees soon blocked his companions from sight, and after another few paces the sound of their voices was fading away. In minutes he could be out of earshot, more alone than a town dweller would ever be.

Or at least, further away from other people. In the woods you're never *truly* alone.

Unfortunately, when Hugh slipped out of camp on August 20, 1823 and headed into the forest with his rifle, he unknowingly set a course straight for one of the most dangerous of all North American animals. The grizzly bear is the biggest bear in the western hemisphere, and while coastal populations reach the largest sizes the ones in the Midwest were still huge. The average female in the region weighed 300 pounds. Unlike the more widespread black bear the grizzly is a significant predator; while it's still an omnivore it likes a lot more meat in its diet, so it's far more willing to get into conflict with another animal. It's also too big to escape easily by climbing trees, so when threatened it usually chooses to fight. Luckily for the grizzly it's a formidable animal, often standing more than nine feet high when it rears up on its hind legs. Its huge paws are armed with lethal six-inch talons and it has one of the most powerful bites of any land animal. Even a mountain lion will rarely stand up to a grizzly; big cats or wolf packs steer clear of them unless they're old or sick. In turn, grizzlies generally leave other predators alone. Their favorite prey is small animals like squirrels, or insect colonies – Yellowstone grizzlies often eat up to 40,000 moths a day. They fish, catching so many salmon that the parts they discard fertilize the forests. Normally they don't bother larger animals, and that includes humans. Most problems occur when bears come foraging round campsites to steal food, but the most dangerous situation is when a hunter stumbles on a mother grizzly with her cubs. That's what Hugh Glass was about to do.

Grizzlies live a long time, around 25 years in the wild, and like most long-lived animals they don't breed often. An adult female usually gives birth every four or five years, and generally has two cubs (although it can be one, or as many as four). The cubs are born in their mother's winter den while she's still hibernating and stay with her for two years, by which time they've grown from about a pound at birth to nearly a hundred times that. In August of their first year they're around 25 pounds and still not really capable of looking after themselves. This makes mother grizzlies fiercely protective. Threaten her cubs and she'll fight to the death – probably yours.

Hugh was stalking quietly through the woods, his rifle at the ready, when he came across the grizzly family. With his backwoods skills the sight of the two cubs, each the size of a small dog, capering and play-fighting in the small clearing would have warned him instantly of the danger he was in. But it was already too late to back quietly away. Before he could reach there was a bellow of rage and the mother bear erupted from the forest, charging straight at him with her huge jaws gaping.

Modern rifles are light and handy; they can be carried safely but made ready to fire with a flick of the safety catch. Hugh's muzzle loader was a completely different beast. To throw its soft lead ball accurately it needed a long, heavy barrel. It also used a delicate and temperamental percussion cap system; for safety, the hammer usually rested at "half-cock", locked in a position where its flat head was slightly raised above the thin copper cap that would fire the powder charge. Before firing the hammer had to be pulled back to full cock against the tension of the mainspring. For a veteran hunter like Hugh it was normally the work of a second to thumb it back until the retaining sear caught it with a heavy click, but it wasn't so easy when at the same time he was frantically bringing the heavy weapon up to face a charging bear. As the hammer snapped into place the roaring grizzly brought a muscled foreleg scything round, and her huge paw caught the rifle's barrel squarely. The gun boomed as it was wrenched from his grip, the ball whirring uselessly into the sky.

Hugh staggered backwards and groped at his belt. Even if he could recover the rifle it would take him a full minute to reload, and he didn't have that time. Instead he drew his heavy horse pistol. Another single-shot muzzle loader, it had a much shorter range than the rifle – its smoothbore barrel made it almost useless beyond about twenty feet – but if he managed to put the ball into the grizzly it would at least slow it down. Antique weapons seem crude compared to modern ones but their massive, heavy projectiles could do horrific damage at close range. High quality balls were usually hardened with mercury to preserve their shape, but the handmade projectiles used by the Mountain Men were just soft lead. On impact they mushroomed into lethal disks that tore savagely into their target. As the bear came on he cocked the clumsy gun and raised it, but again the bear lashed out. This time her four-inch claws raked his arm, slicing deeply into the flesh. The pistol spun away into the brush, unfired. Then the bear was on him.

The first charge threw Glass sprawling to the ground, bleeding from claw wounds to the chest and arms. He rolled desperately away, scrabbling for his last weapon – his knife – as the grizzly came at him again. This time it sank its teeth into his shoulder, worrying at him like a huge dog and shredding the flesh of his shoulder and back. A grizzly has the strongest bite of any American mammal. Its jaws are powerful enough to crush a bowling ball,[v] let alone any bone in the human body. Hugh was just lucky it had fastened its teeth in his flesh and missed the shoulder blade, but even so it was a grievous wound. As the bear dragged him across the clearing towards the hungry cubs he knew he had little time left to get away. As his knife came free of the sheath he didn't hesitate; he twisted round and drove the foot of sharpened steel into her flank.

Instantly the bear, roaring furiously, released her grip and swiped at him again with her paws. The slamming blows tore open his scalp and badly gashed his neck. Somehow he managed to keep hold of the knife and stabbed her again, and again. She backed off for a moment and the battered Mountain Man dragged himself to his feet and started backing away, the dripping blade held ready to lunge. The bear wasn't ready to let him go, however. Again she rushed at him and her jaws clamped shut on his leg. He felt the bone snap under the pressure but, gritting his teeth, plunged the knife in to her back, angling it between the ribs. When the hilt slammed against her rough pelt he dragged it out and drove it in again. Then she yanked his leg out from under him and he fell once more.

Sprawled on the carpet of dead leaves with blood pouring from a dozen deep wounds, Hugh was in a bad way. But as the bear came at him again she was weakening, too. The repeated rip of the long, broad knife had perforated her lungs and blood was quickly draining into her chest. As she started forward she sneezed a spray of bright arterial blood, and her movements were slower, less certain. Still, once again she lashed out with her great paws. Hugh felt the skin and muscle on his other leg sheared open, then she came at his throat with those crushing jaws agape for a final bite. He threw one arm around her neck, hugging himself close in an attempt to avoid her claws, and thumped the knife home again. And again. More hot blood washed over his hand. The bear staggered and took a step back, but his own strength was fading now. As the grizzly batted weakly at him, opening another row of gashes, he thrust the knife into her chest one more time then slumped to the ground. The bear shook her head tiredly, spraying blood, then swayed drunkenly on her feet. She pawed feebly at the bone handle projecting between her ribs then gave a last tired grunt and collapsed over the bleeding trapper. Moments later a rescue party, alerted by the boom of Hugh's rifle and the grizzly's angry roars, rushed out of the trees.

It was a horrific sight. Hugh lay on his back, soaked in blood and unconscious. One leg skewed away at an impossible angle and torn clothing revealed a shoulder mangled into a dripping mess of torn meat. The bear sprawled half across his torso, still moving feebly, the silvered brown fur drenched into long streaks of glistening black. One of the men ran to the animal, placed the muzzle of his rifle against her skull and pulled the trigger. The grizzly stiffened then sagged, and the others quickly dragged the carcass off their companion. The cubs, already doomed to starvation by their mother's death, whined in terror until the vengeful trappers shot them. The bears were all dead, but as the men gathered around Hugh's tattered form it seemed obvious he would soon be joining them.

The Mountain Men were used to death. Most expeditions claimed their tragic toll, whether through animal attacks, weather or disease. This one had already lost plenty of men to the weapons of the Arikara. Even so, it was a shock to see a tall, strong and experienced man like Hugh reduced to this condition. Every man among them knew that he might not come back. Death in the wilderness was a risk they had confronted and accepted. Still, it was also something to be avoided where possible. The first thing was to see if anything could be done for their wounded comrade.

The answer wasn't a hopeful one. Some accounts say that Hugh had at least fifteen separate wounds, covering every major part of his body. His back had been so badly torn by the grizzly's bite that his ribs could be seen, glistening through a film of blood. Deep gashes scored his chest, limbs and scalp. The broken leg, itself a disabling and life-threatening mutilation, was probably the least of his problems. The real danger, if he didn't bleed to death in front of their eyes, was infection.

Chapter 6

Any wound can potentially let dangerous microorganisms into the body, resulting in an infection. Today we can usually control these infections with antibiotics, but before the 1930s there was little that could be done. Many people succumbed to what would now be minor injuries, and surgery was incredibly dangerous. When Ignatz Semmelweiss deduced that contamination could be passed by dirty hands and instruments the risk went down, and antiseptics helped even more, but once a wound had become infected it became a waiting game to see if the patient would live or die. Injuries from animals were particularly dreaded. A predator – and although the grizzly is omnivorous it does hunt and eat meat – collects tiny fragments of flesh and blood around its teeth and claws. These are a perfect breeding ground for dangerous bacteria, and when the animal attacks this contamination is driven deep into the wounds it inflicts. That's why a bird or mouse captured by a cat is almost inevitably doomed even if released alive – the teeth just have to break the skin to inject a potentially lethal infection. The grizzly had done a lot more than break Hugh's skin. His injuries were shocking, and dirty. In addition to residue from the bear itself the gashed and mangled flesh was riddled with soil and torn fragments of his clothing, which after months in the wilderness wasn't as clean as it might have been. It would be a miracle if none of the injuries turned red and started to swell, and if that happened the likely result was sepsis – blood poisoning, a rampaging tide of corruption that would finally attack every one of his organs and lead to an agonizing, fevered death.

It must have occurred to some of them that it would be kinder to put a rifle to Hugh's head and pull the trigger, but that was a hard step to take. Instead, Major Henry decided to treat him as well as they could and see what happened. There were limits to what they could do. The wounds could be washed, and any visible debris picked out. Perhaps one of them had experience of suturing, and tried to close the larger gashes with fine strands of sinew or silk thread. A splash of whiskey would have been agonizing, but reasonably effective at sterilizing a wound. With his wounds roughly dressed – and for bandages they usually used dirty strips of the wounded man's shirt - all they could really do next was make Hugh as comfortable as they could and wait to see what happened.

Henry didn't want to wait, though. They had to get on to the fort, and while it was only August the weather would start closing in on them within weeks. It was vital to keep moving. They waited one night by the scene of the attack, half expecting him to be dead by morning, but when the sun rose above the trees he still lived. It was time to press on. Henry ordered the men to make a litter from stripped branches and they carried Glass with them, moaning and writhing in pain, for two days. Most of them expected him to succumb at some point in the arduous journey, but he stubbornly clung to life. Unfortunately the litter was slowing them down, not so much because of its weight but because they had to move carefully to avoid jarring the wounded man too badly. Finally it was obvious that if they had to carry him all the way, winter would be on them not long after they finally reached the fort. Their slower pace also made them more vulnerable to Indian attacks. It was time for a difficult decision.

Examining Hugh, Major Henry was more convinced than ever he couldn't survive. His wounds were barely healing, the first hints of infection were already visible in the seeping gashes, and his broken leg was suffering agonies from the bumping of the makeshift stretcher. It could only be a matter of days, and probably very few of them. With a heavy heart he announced they would have to leave him behind.

They couldn't just abandon him though. Unless they were willing to finish him off, which they weren't, someone would have to stay with him until he died then give him a decent burial. That had risks of its own, of course, but they were manageable. The group was hunting and exploring as it went and a couple of men moving as fast as they could should be able to catch up after waiting a few days. When they stopped by a small stream sheltered by a grove of trees Henry asked for volunteers. It had risks, he explained, but they weren't too serious and old Hugh deserved a decent grave. In gratitude the company would pay a generous bonus – worth several months' wages – to two men who stayed behind until the inevitable happened.[vi]

That was a difficult offer to think about. Every man in the company knew the dangers presented by the Arikara tribe, because they'd dug enough graves already on their long journey. If anyone hadn't appreciated the equally serious risks of wild animals, Hugh's mangled body was enough to make the point. Even so, the money was tempting. Almost without exception they were there to seek their fortunes, and what Henry was offering would make a huge difference to their profits from the trip. For long minutes they sat, pondering the choice, while Henry waited and Hugh Glass groaned on his litter. Then one man nodded. "I'll do it," he said. Moments later another joined him. "Me too."

The older of the two volunteers was John Fitzgerald; the other was Jim Bridger, one of the youngest in the whole party at only nineteen years old. Despite his youth Bridger was the man of his family; his income had to support both himself and his younger sister. That's probably what decided him on staying. Fitzgerald's motivations are unknown. One legend has it that the two men fell asleep on sentry duty one night and Glass, finding them, earned their gratitude by not reporting them to Major Henry. That seems fanciful, though, in reality both were probably motivated by the money and a sense of loyalty.

With the decision made, Henry issued his orders. The two men were to stay with Glass until he recovered or (much more likely) died. When he died they were to give him a proper burial then catch up with the main group as quickly as they could. In the meantime they should stay quiet and inconspicuous to avoid attracting the attention of any war parties. The Arikara were still the main threat, but one recent attack that had killed two men turned out to have been the work of the Handan. Although closely related to the Arikara this tribe had been friendly up until now, and Henry was worried that the Arikara's attacks on his party had emboldened hotheads among the other tribes. From now on any Indians they met would have to be seen as at least potentially hostile; that was going to make things much more dangerous for the two men left behind. They had their own weapons for self-defense but two muzzle-loading rifles weren't much of a deterrent to a large group of warriors. They certainly didn't want to attract attention by hunting with the guns, so a supply of rations was left with them. They could supplement these stores by foraging for edible roots and berries but gunshots were to be avoided if at all possible. Even a fire would be a risk. On the other hand the stream was clean, fresh water that could be drunk without boiling; it rose from a spring within yards of where Glass lay. Apart from the guns and food all they had were a couple of digging tools for when the time came to dig a grave. Henry took a few minutes to give them all the helpful tips he could, reassured them that they'd be able to catch up on the route he explained to them, then ordered the rest of the group to move out. The column of trappers shouldered their loads of bedding, pelts, food and weapons, and tramped away north into the vast, forbidding wilderness. Within minutes they were gone from sight. Fitzgerald and Bridger were alone with the dying man.

Chapter 7

At first it wasn't too bad. There was little they could do for Hugh apart from sponge his head with cool stream water to fight his rising fever, and it seemed inevitable that he would die within hours. They started work on a grave, digging as quietly as they could, but when the sun started to set they left the shallow pit unfinished and sat watching the shadows lengthen. Perhaps on that first night they could see the smoke of their companions' campfire a few miles to the north, rising above the darkening forest. Perhaps an occasional yellow flicker reached them from a distant hillside through the night. Around them in the grove all was dark and still – but not silent. They could hear the scurry of night animals in the forest, and the sudden burst of violence as some unseen predator struck. They heard the wind sighing in the leaves above, and the tinkling of the little stream. And always there were the mutters and moans of Hugh Glass, their maimed companion who stubbornly refused to die.

When the sun came up next day Hugh still lived. His wounds were starting to stink as the infection sank deeper into them, his fever was more intense and his movements weaker, but he hadn't died in the night. All that day they tended him, waiting for his torment to end. But when night approached again he still lived. Surely, they thought, he'll be gone by morning? He wasn't. As the dawn broke on the second day he was still with them – weaker, more pain-wracked, but still alive.

On the third dawn he still lived. And the fourth. And the fifth. Finally Fitzgerald began to buckle under the strain. More experienced than young Bridger, he understood how dangerous their situation was. As time passed the trail of the main body was fading. Henry had told them the route they'd be taking but it wasn't like giving directions today; there were no named or numbered routes to follow. The expedition's track could wander a couple of miles, or even more, each side of the route Henry had explained. It would be quite possible for them to miss the group and wander, lost, through the wilderness. The risk was low as long as they had a clear trail to follow but that was fading by the hour. As they sat by the almost-comatose Glass footprints were being eroded away by the wind, crushed grass was straightening again and the fresh ends of broken twigs were weathering into invisibility. The longer they waited the harder it would be to follow their companions – and the higher the chances of an Arikara raiding party finding them. As the fifth day passed, Fitzgerald started laying out the case for moving on.

At first Bridger probably resisted. They'd agreed to stay with Glass until he died, and he hadn't, quite. True, he was quieter now, his iron strength seemingly fading away finally, but he still clung to a thread of life. Once again, the thought must have occurred: wouldn't it be kinder to use a rifle to end his pain? But firing a shot could bring Indians down on them; it was too much of a risk. They could finish him with a knife, but neither of them had the stomach for that. Finally they came to a deal. They'd wait one more night with Hugh, and if he died before the sun came up they'd finish the grave they'd started and give him a Christian burial in it. If he was still alive… they'd leave him to take his chances, and set off after Henry's party.

When the sun rose on the sixth day Glass was still alive. He was deep in fever now, his breathing just a hoarse rasp that barely lifted his torn chest, but he hadn't let go his tenuous hold on life. The two men looked at each other, filled with misgivings. Neither of them really wanted to do this, but nor did they want to stay here any longer. If they set off right now they'd have the whole day to travel in and they could start making up some of the ground they'd lost here. If they waited yet another day, who knew what might happen? When Henry had asked them to stay here he probably expected it to be for a day or two, no longer. Now it had been nearly a week. Their rations were running dangerously low – if they waited much longer they'd have to start hunting, with all the dangers that carried. Fitzgerald was convinced it was time to move on and Bridger, more reluctantly, agreed.

But what to do with Glass? The thought of burying him alive revolted them, but they didn't want to just leave him where he lay either. Surely he'd die soon. Maybe they also worried what would happen if someone else from the party came this way again, and found his picked bones lying beside a half-dug grave. Finally they laid him in the shallow pit, covered him with the pelt of the grizzly and filled in the pit with twigs and leaves. Now he was sort of buried, but the last sparks of life wouldn't be snuffed out by a choking layer of earth.

Before they left they collected up the dying man's equipment. The Mountain Men traveled light on personal comforts, so there wasn't much. A necessities pouch with a flint and steel, sewing kit and a few other small items. His pistol. The big knife that had served him so well in his fight with the grizzly. His shot bag and powder flask. Finally, his rifle. It's often said that Hugh Glass carried one of the famous Hawken rifles, but he didn't; the Hawken brothers made their first weapons in 1823, when Hugh was already far into the wilderness. What we do know is that whatever kind of rifle it was, he treasured it. We can also guess that it was a better weapon than the one Fitzgerald was carrying, because now he picked it up and loaded it. His own rifle was slung over his back; none of them would ever leave a firearm behind. Guns were just too valuable out here. Finally they shouldered the bags with their remaining food, and with troubled glances back at the small grove they set off on the trail of the main party.

Within a week Fitzgerald and Bridger had caught up with Henry's men and related the story of Hugh Glass's death and burial. The other men accepted the tale without question. After all it was more than believable; it was exactly what they'd expected to hear. All that surprised them was that he'd held on so long before dying. Reunited, the group headed on towards Fort Henry.

But a hundred miles behind them the fires of vengeance were burning. Sometime after they'd abandoned him – perhaps two or three days later, perhaps while they were still within earshot – the fever that gripped Hugh had receded slightly and he'd once more become aware of his surroundings. At first it was all he could do to drag himself out of the pit they'd laid him in. Weak, crippled and perched on the edge of death's abyss he could do no more than scoop a few handfuls of water from the stream and pick low-hanging berries. For days he lay there, slipping in and out of consciousness. Then came a time when he opened his eyes and saw a rattlesnake just feet from him, slow and lazy, warming itself in the late summer sun. Perhaps he should have felt fear; in his condition, one bite from the big snake would have finished him off in minutes. Instead it was another word that swam up in his mind. *Food*. Scrabbling quietly in the forest floor he found a fist-sized rock and writhed slowly forward. The snake turned its blank eyes towards him and gave a warning hiss, but Hugh ignored it. Gathering the dregs of his strength he made a sudden lunge, slamming the rock down and feeling the snake's head crush beneath it. The muscular body writhed and twitched for a few minutes, then lay still. So did Hugh, utterly drained by the effort needed to strike, but finally he could move again. This time he searched for a sharp-edged flake of rock.

Eventually he found a crude stone tool and began skinning the snake's carcass. Then he shaved away tiny slivers of flesh and, one by one, swallowed them raw. With each morsel he could feel strength beginning to return. He sliced and ate, sliced and ate; eventually the whole snake was gone. Now he felt well enough to consider his situation.

He'd already tried to stand, and knew it was impossible. He couldn't walk. Right now he was so weak he couldn't even *crawl*; the best he could manage was to slowly inch his body forward like a worm. There was no way he could hope to catch up with the group. No, his priority had to be getting out of the wilderness and finding men who could treat his wounds. Then, when he was well again, he could set about tracking down the men who had left him here to die. The big question was, what direction should he go? Finally he decided to head for Fort Kiowa, to the southeast. The problem was it was a long way to the southeast – especially for a man who could move barely ten yards in an hour. That didn't matter to him. Wrapping himself in the bearskin for some protection, he looked around for a landmark that would guide him to the Cheyenne River. Finally he settled on the 2,733 foot summit of Thunder Butte. That lay in the right direction and it was impossible to miss. He took a last look around the grove, wriggled to face the butte and started inching his way forward.

Chapter 8

At first he barely covered any ground. His wounds had weakened him almost to helplessness, and he knew it was only a matter of time before infection killed him. The broken leg was also a crippling handicap. Finally he managed to set the bone and bind it up with a splint. There was no way he could walk on it but now it didn't cause a new flare of agony with every movement, and if he'd done it right the bone might even start to heal. Next he had to deal with the corruption that was sinking into his torn flesh. Remembering a piece of old Indian lore, next time he came across the decaying corpse of an animal he gritted his teeth and lay in the stinking mess. Maggots writhed across the bones and he felt them work their way into his own wounds.

Maggot therapy sounds disgusting, but it's been used since ancient times and was very popular during the Napoleonic Wars and the Civil War. The larvae of some types of flies only eat dead flesh, not living tissue. It was that dead flesh that was rotting and poisoning Hugh's wounds. Now the maggots began munching away at it. The feeling was loathsome at first, but as days passed the wounds became cleaner and the poisoning began to recede. Slowly he gained more strength. His diet was poor, and without his knowledge of the woods he would have starved to death, but by digging up edible roots and fungi, and stripping berries from low-hanging branches, he managed to scavenge enough calories to keep going. In fact he was going faster now. As his body started to heal he managed to crawl properly, and his rate of progress increased to several yards a minute. He passed out less often, and the towering butte slowly came closer. Now he was covering up to a mile a day, then a little more.

Sometime in the middle of September he crawled into the territory of a wolfpack. It must have been terrifying to hear their howls in the night as he huddled, wrapped in the bearskin for warmth, under the low branches of some tree. Wolves don't attack people often but it's not exactly unknown either, and in his weakened condition he had no chance of fighting off a pack. But when he did encounter them he somehow managed to turn the tables. As he crawled on, he came across the freshly killed carcass of a young bison with two wolves gorging themselves on it. Most men would have slunk away back into the shelter of the forest, but not Hugh. Amazingly he frightened the wolves away from their kill and dragged himself across to it. He'd been living on plants, grubs, insects and anything small that came within reach of his hands, but now here were pounds of raw but energy-rich meat. He made the most of the opportunity, eating the tender heart and liver then gnawing off as much as he could stomach. He had no way to take much with him, because without salt to preserve it or a fire to smoke it decay would make it inedible within days, but while he had the chance he stuffed himself. Then he crawled on.

Towards the end of September he reached the Cheyenne River. Incredibly he had covered a hundred miles in less than a month, with no equipment and a broken leg. Fall was closing in though, and the nights were becoming cold. He knew that he'd have to make faster progress if he wasn't going to be caught out here when winter came. The river offered that prospect. Finding a dead tree, he managed to lash together a crude raft and floated himself out into the stream. Days later the Cheyenne carried him into the Missouri River, on course for Fort Kiowa.

Using the river was dangerous, because the Arikara built their villages along it and there was a chance of him being spotted and attacked, but his luck held even when he went ashore to forage. Finally he had drifted all the way back to the village the expedition had burned after the attack in June. It was abandoned now, the Arikara having left for their winter hunting grounds, and he decided to go ashore and search for food. He was lucky; in one of the burned huts he found a corn store, and he was able to clear the ash away and dig out a supply of edible corn. Now he was able to hobble, keeping himself upright with a rough crutch – but he was still in a bad way. It was incredible that he'd made it this far; only his determination had carried him down to the Missouri again. Perhaps that determination impressed the Sioux foraging party who found him as he searched through the deserted village. The Sioux often picked over Arikara lands when they moved for the winter, searching the lodges and fields for any overlooked corn. Now they found this strange, half-crippled white man. The Sioux were an unpredictable tribe. Nomadic, they didn't farm like the Arikara. Instead they relied on hunting, foraging and pillaging the crops of the settled farmers. They were also notable warriors, who had quickly mastered combat on horseback, and were one of the most feared tribes. However they were also capable of great kindness, and the party who had found Hugh seemed to think he had already suffered enough. They treated his wounds as well as they could, even sewing a piece of bearskin to his back to cover the still-open wound there.[vii] Then they let him ride with them for several days as they headed downriver. After that he limped on, alone, with his crutch. Near the end of October, he finally walked up to the gates of Fort Kiowa.

Fort Kiowa was a French fur post, competitors of Ashley and Henry's company, but there were arrangements between the fur companies. They might be rivals but they all worked out in a hostile land, and where necessary they looked after each other. Hugh was taken in at the fort, and his wounds cleaned and treated more professionally. In fact, most of them were well on their way to healing by now, including his broken leg, but his back was still very serious. Now, cleaner conditions and a regular diet helped it improve. Meanwhile, he was able to use company credit to re-equip himself from the fort's small store. New clothes replaced his stinking rags, and he picked up a replacement rifle and knife.

He must have had a truly iron constitution. Not only had he survived his wounds, he'd actually managed to recover much of his strength while scrabbling through the wilderness. Now he was getting better rapidly, but it was still almost a month before he was fit enough to leave the fort again. When he did there was only one thought in his mind: revenge. Now that he was able to get around he intended to hunt down and kill the two men who had left him in the woods to die. Luckily for him he knew exactly where they had been heading. Fort Henry, back the way he had come.

In mid-November Hugh set out in a pirogue, a lightweight flat-bottomed boat popular with trappers along the Midwestern rivers, with a party of six French hunters. The French were planning a hunting trip further up the river; Hugh was hitching a ride as far as he could on his journey to Fort Henry. There was less urgency now, because according to the plan the expedition would be spending the winter at the fort, but he had just gone through an incredible ordeal and if he could avoid a couple hundred miles of walking that was just fine. He was also propelled forward by his anger, so the faster he could reach the confrontation with Fitzgerald and Bridger the happier he would be.

Unfortunately for Hugh, he wasn't the only one with scores to settle. The Arikara were still angry at the white interlopers and the sight of such a small party making their way upriver infuriated them. It wasn't long before the pirogue was being watched on its way up the Missouri. Within days a trap was arranged, and sprung.

Of the seven men, five were in the pirogue when the Arikara attacked. Their interpreter, Toussaint Charbonneau, had gone on ahead to talk to the local Mandan Indians. Hugh was on shore hunting. The others were caught completely by surprise, and overwhelmed by a sudden volley of musket balls and arrows. As they lay bleeding and wounded in the boat the warriors were already in the water, swimming towards them with scalping knives clutched in their hands. None of the five escaped.

Hugh also had a narrow escape. Most of the Arikara were concentrating on the boat, but a small scouting party stumbled on him as he fled from the scene of the massacre. His wounded leg was still slowing him down and he was almost caught, but then the Mandan intervened. They also had a scouting party in the area, and a group of Mandan warriors rescued him. They were mounted and one of them hoisted the Mountain Man over his saddle before galloping away to safety. They released him when they were beyond pursuit and he continued his journey alone, while Charbonneau made his way back to Fort Kiowa. Glass headed in the other direction and on November 20 he reached Fort Tilton, a Columbia Fur Company post further up the Missouri River. The trappers there were getting settled in for winter and there wasn't a lot they could do to help him but they did take him across the river, reckoning he was less likely to meet more Arikara on the other bank.

It was 250 miles from Fort Tilton to his destination and the weather was bad now. Snow-laden winds whipped through the hills and forests, making progress difficult and bone-chillingly cold. Hugh struggled on, drawing on every bit of his strength and skill to survive the winter trek. He hunted when he could, despite the noise of his shots. There was no choice; he needed food to survive. Where edible plants showed above the snow he foraged them. Through each day he struggled on, staying in the more sheltered valleys when he could and only taking to the high ground to avoid scouting Indians. The meager rations he'd brought from Fort Tilton were soon gone and he was entirely on his own resources. But he was determined. Day by day he covered the miles, pushing hard as the temperatures fell and the snow deepened. Despite the conditions he still averaged close to ten miles a day, and about ten days before Christmas he saw the walls of Fort Henry across the river.

His first view of the fort kindled a dreadful suspicion, but he'd come this far; he was going to get across the Missouri and cover the final yards. Two logs and some birch bark lashings provided him with a crude raft. Lying precariously on the tiny craft he pushed out into the stream, paddling with the butt of his rifle. It was a slow crossing because he had to be careful not to overbalance. Tough as he was, if falling into the icy water didn't kill him from shock he'd die of hypothermia before he could hope to light a fire and warm himself again. On he paddled, steadily working the cold gun alternately on each side. After long minutes the bow of the raft bumped the opposite bank and he reached out with a frozen hand. Gripping a clump of dead grass he pulled the raft securely against the shore and rolled off onto dry land. Then, brushing bark and snow from his coat, he picked up his few belongings and approached the gate of the outpost. Before he reached it his suspicions were confirmed. Fort Henry was deserted.

Chapter 9

There were all sorts of reasons the fort could have been abandoned, from Indian attack to an outbreak of disease, but after poking around the empty stores and bunkhouse Hugh realized that the party had pushed further to the northwest. Major Henry had left a message painted on a wall for anyone who came after them – although this was one person he would never have expected to see it – to say that they were moving on up the Yellowstone to establish a new base for the winter. That was enough for Hugh. He rested out of the wind for a few hours while his clothes dried over a fire, and then he set out in pursuit once more. He was still on the right track; he knew he could catch up.

And he was right. It took him another two weeks, pushing on at an incredible pace through savage blizzards and shivering in snow caves each bitterly cold night, and he covered close to 200 miles. Then, on the last day of December, he found his goal where the Bighorn River flowed into the Yellowstone.[viii] The group had built a new fort, a stockade of sharpened trunks driven deep into the cold earth with a small cluster of huts inside. It was nothing like the big US Army forts depicted in a hundred Westerns, with elaborate fighting platforms along the walls, but it would serve to defend the trappers from animals and small raiding parties as they hunkered down to sit out the cold weather. In building it the company had cleared the trees for a radius of a hundred yards then cut back the brush to leave a circle of bare ground that would let them see anyone approaching. Now a couple of sentries guarded the gate against any sudden rush of attacking Indians. As 1823's last dusk fell Hugh trudged out of the forest's gathering shadows and made his way up to the gate.

All the sentries would have seen was a man in a buckskin coat and felt hat, with a bundle and a rifle slung over his shoulders. Mountain Men often adopted items of Indian dress, like beaten silver ornaments, or feathers in their hats, while many Indians had taken to wearing broad-brimmed hats. Hugh's own affectation by this time was a necklace of bear teeth. At first it would have been hard to identify him as a white man as he approached from the gloom and the sentries probably fingered their rifles nervously, but as he came closer they saw his bushy beard and recognized him as a fellow European. Then, with dawning incredulity, they realized his features were familiar. One of them stammered, "Hey, is it really you?"

"Yeah, it's me. I'm here to kill those sonsabitches Fitzgerald and Bridger."

There wasn't much to say to that. They hauled the gate open and led him inside. "You better talk to the Major."

Since he'd been abandoned in the forest Hugh had squirmed, crawled, hobbled, floated and walked close to 700 miles. Every inch of that way he'd been driven on by the thought of vengeance against the two men who'd left him in the grove to die. Now, he thought, that moment was here. His rifle was loaded and primed; he dipped his right shoulder and deftly caught the weapon as its strap slipped loose. He'd blow a hole in the first of them then go after the other with his knife. Then as they approached the fort's bunkhouse one of his escorts announced his presence with a shout; "Hugh Glass is here! He's alive!" Inside the log hut there was a sudden silence. A moment later the door was thrown open and Major Andrew Henry stood in the rectangle of yellow lamplight.

Henry was stunned into silence for a moment. He was face to face with a man he'd believed dead these last four months, and now here he was. The figure in front of him was battered, gaunt and exhausted but it was unmistakably Hugh Glass, who Fitzgerald and Bridger had assured him was dead and buried. His mind raced. If those two had abandoned Glass to die he would probably be seeking vengeance, and the sight of the cocked rifle in his hands confirmed that fear. Henry understood. In the trapper's position he'd have felt exactly the same. He couldn't let it happen, though. Not for legal reasons – it would be murder of course, but the Mountain Men had their own code and the lethal retribution Glass wanted would be close enough to justice in their eyes. Henry could live with that, but his party had lost enough men already and now there were less than a dozen of them left. He couldn't let that number be reduced further. He thought quickly.

When Hugh made to push past him into the bunkhouse Henry blocked his path. "Hang on Hugh, I'll get young Bridger out here, but first you sling that rifle."

For a moment it looked like Hugh was going to argue, then his eyes shifted and Henry heard footsteps on the wooden floor behind him. A moment later came a gasp of astonishment. "Oh my God, you're alive." Henry turned to see Jim Bridger standing there, white as a sheet and with a strange mixture of relief and terror on his face. The young man took a hesitant step forward even as Glass leveled the rifle at his hip and pulled back the hammer. "I told him it was wrong to leave you like that. My God, it's good to see you here!"

Hugh's finger was already tightening on the trigger to send a ball spinning into Bridger's chest, but now he hesitated. Memories swam up, fragments of argument overheard while he was deep in the fever dreams. Yes, that could be true. He remembered the young man's reluctance, and Fitzgerald's increasingly frequent urgings. Bridger took another step towards him; the rifle's muzzle wavered. He stared into the teenager's face. No, this was barely more than a boy. The hard life out here had already pushed him to the limit and he couldn't be blamed for giving in to the pressure and following the older man's lead. Slowly Hugh dropped the muzzle to point at the trampled snow, then gripped the hammer in his left hand and pulled the trigger. He lowered the hammer slowly until it clicked safely back into the half cock position. Henry said quietly, "Well done Hugh. Now shake on it."

Inside the bunkhouse the men were seeing in the New Year with a small keg of whiskey. Hugh, his gear dumped on an empty bunk and his heavy outer layers stripped away, settled gratefully into the circle around the crude woodstove and someone pressed a tin cup of liquor into his hand. As his stiff muscles began to ease in the warmth he heard the story of what had happened since his battle with the grizzly. When Fitzgerald and a subdued Bridger had rejoined the group carrying his gear nobody had any reason to doubt that he had died; it was what they had been expecting. Hugh could understand that, because he was as surprised as anyone else that he'd managed to survive. Now that he was back with them there was general rejoicing that he'd made it through, and anger at those who had abandoned him – although if Hugh was willing to forgive Bridger, so was everyone else. Fitzgerald was different though. Fitzgerald was the one who had come up with the idea of leaving him in the woods to die. Fitzgerald was the one who'd persuaded

Bridger to run out on him. Fitzgerald was the one who'd stolen his rifle and spun the lies about his death. Fitzgerald was old and experienced enough to know better.

But Fitzgerald was gone.

He was still determined to kill the older man, but he'd missed him by weeks. In mid-November, around the time Glass was leaving Fort Kiowa, Fitzgerald had decided he'd had enough of the expedition and set out back east with two other men. They'd built a small boat and paddled away down the Missouri River. Somewhere along the way, perhaps while Hugh was with the Mandan who'd rescued him from the last ambush, their paths had crossed without meeting.[ix]

The problem was that although the men knew where Fitzgerald had headed – Fort Atkinson, at Council Bluff in eastern Nebraska – winter was now here in earnest and there was no question of setting out in pursuit. He was going to have to stay at the fort until the weather started to improve in spring. The final decision on that was up to Henry and he wasn't completely enthusiastic. He seems to have been angry at what Fitzgerald and Bridger had done, but at the same time he at least partly blamed Glass for his predicament.[x] If he hadn't constantly roamed away from the group he might never have been mauled so badly, and the days of carrying him on the litter had endangered the rest of the men. Still, he'd been one of the group right from the start and the men had welcomed him back. At the end of the day that was enough for Henry. The small group settled in for the winter and Hugh Glass settled in with them.

It was a hard season. Winter in eastern Montana is no place for the weak, and just staying alive was a challenge. Like all long-term trapping expeditions they were living off the land. By now even their reserves of flour were almost depleted; they'd traded with the Indians to buy cornflour and were mixing that with ground spruce and pine bark to stretch it out further. Greens were at a premium, as was meat, and a skilled woodsman like Hugh was able to pay his way just by the food he brought in. Then of course he was an extra pair of hands to gather fuel. For the first two months of the new year the little fort was swept by vicious blizzards, piling up feet of snow. Temperatures plunged to zero overnight, and through January never rose above freezing even at noon. The little stove burned tons of firewood that winter and every man hauled his share of it. Preserving the warmth in the bunkhouse was a constant effort, and between that and keeping themselves fed there was little time to brood on thoughts of revenge.

In March the weather began to ease. By mid-morning meltwater was dripping from the roofs of the huts, and days at a time passed with no fresh snowfall. The ice that choked the Yellowstone began to clear. Blue sky began to appear again through the clouds. Eventually Hugh decided he was willing to take his chances and set out after Fitzgerald. Henry agreed; he planned to send a small party to St. Louis to let Ashley know the group had survived the winter, and he picked Glass as one of their number. On March 27 they set off on the thousand-mile journey back to Missouri.[xi] There were five of them: Dutton, More, Chapman, Marsh and Glass. The ice in the Yellowstone was still too treacherous for them to travel by boat, so they set off overland towards the Platte River. Reaching it they shot and skinned two bison. After gorging themselves on fresh meat grilled over a fire they made two frames from green branches and covered them with the bison hides to make a pair of small but serviceable boats. Paddles were cut from larger branches, and they started off down the river; the plan was to follow the Platte to the Missouri, which would take them close to Fort Atkinson then on to the Mississippi and St. Louis.

They didn't make it. Close to where the Laramie River joins the Platte they came across an Indian winter encampment. Thinking it was a Pawnee village they paddled to shore and tried to trade for more food. At first it went well, then Hugh realized that the language he was hearing wasn't exactly like the Pawnee he barely understood – but it was familiar all the same. "These are Rickarees!" he yelled, and ran for the river bank. The others followed, but Chapman and Moore were quickly caught and killed. Dutton had stayed to watch the boats and managed to paddle out into the stream and escape; Marsh got away down the bank and managed to stay ahead of his pursuers long enough to attract Dutton's attention and be rescued. Hugh, who'd swum the river to get away, watched them go. Once more he was alone in hostile territory, and his only weapon was his knife; he'd had to abandon the rifle as he swam. Still, he was better off than he'd been last time. Undaunted, he crept away from the Arikara village then set out towards Fort Kiowa.

By this time Glass had a reputation among the tribes of the Midwest; news of his repeated escapes from the Arikara had spread widely, and while that made many frontier posts wary of helping him for fear of provoking the tribe it also made him a minor celebrity among their enemies. Hugh himself was confident he could make it back to the fort; in addition to his knife he had his necessities pouch, which contained a fire starting kit and a few other useful tools. Days after his latest escape he met another group of Mandan and they gave him a hand ax. He still had no rifle, but he had all he needed to make traps and forage. Carefully, always alert for another Arikara ambush, he made his way to the fort. Getting there took ten weeks, and though the Frenchmen probably weren't too pleased to see such a notorious tribal enemy they let him in as they had done in October. His credit with Ashley's company was still good, so once more he outfitted himself with a rifle and ammunition at the store and set off towards Fort Atkinson.

Fort Atkinson was no trapping outpost. Founded in 1819, it was the first US Army post west of the Missouri River and by 1823 it had a population of well over 1,000 people. Its permanent garrison was a company of soldiers from the 6th US Infantry, and the military played host to hundreds more civilians – trappers, blacksmiths, storekeepers and others. Instead of a crude log stockade there was a hollow square of barracks, with blank outer walls and ramparts built on their roofs. The fort enclosed more than 150 acres and had a population of over a thousand. Its Army presence was enough to pacify the land for dozens of miles in every direction. In the end, it would pacify Hugh Glass, too.

Hugh reached the fort in early July, and he announced his intentions right away – he wanted to find John Fitzgerald and kill him. The gate sentries asked why; Hugh told them. The soldiers were sympathetic, but they had a job to do; they sent him to the post commander, Captain Bennett C. Riley. Riley was a career Army officer, who would end his 37-year military career in 1850 as a Major General and military governor of California. Right now he was a ten-year veteran Indian fighter, who'd been hardened by dozens of small skirmishes against the hostile tribes. He was familiar with the Mountain Men and their customs, and he could also sympathize with Hugh's story. The tale of abandonment and deceit disgusted him. But John Fitzgerald was now one of his men.

After the success of the War of Independence the founding fathers, inherently suspicious of standing armies, disbanded all except one regiment of the Continental Army and relied on militias for defense. This quickly proved disastrous; in November 1791 a mixed force of regular Army and militia was crushed by a coalition of Miami, Shawnee and Delaware warriors despite having a slight superiority in numbers. The rump army was reorganized into the Legion of the United States and rapidly expanded. In 1796 the name was changed back to United States Army but the expansion continued for decades, and even in 1823 the frontier regiments would eagerly snap up any Mountain Man or pioneer who volunteered. John Fitzgerald had made that step in April and was now part of the US Army. It's not clear whether he had enlisted as a regular or was hired as a scout, but from Captain Riley's point of view it didn't matter. Fitzgerald was on the fort's payroll and protected by military law. He offered Glass a mug of coffee, sat him down and explained to him that if he killed Fitzgerald he would be arrested and hanged by the Army. That was the way it worked; US soldiers couldn't be killed without dire consequences.

Hugh was stunned. After forgiving Bridger he'd traveled hundreds of miles more, and cheated death at the hands of the Arikara yet again, only to be cheated of his last hope of revenge. Riley and the other soldiers at the post understood his anger, but they weren't going to let him kill one of their own even if they were disgusted at what he'd done. Even so, he countered with a different demand. Fitzgerald had stolen his old rifle and he wanted it back. Riley agreed to let him meet Fitzgerald if he gave his word not to harm him, and grudgingly Hugh agreed.

It was not a happy meeting. Hugh had forgiven young Bridger, but this man had gone far beyond what could be atoned for. Bitterly, he demanded his old rifle back. Shaken and humiliated, Fitzgerald handed it over. Glass then berated him for his cowardice and warned him that for his own safety he should never leave the Army. Fitzgerald got the message – if he became a civilian again the Mountain Men would immediately come for him. Finally, disgusted, Hugh turned and walked away. Fitzgerald never saw him again.

John Fitzgerald vanishes from history at that point. What happened to him? It's impossible to say. It's unlikely his remaining time at Fort Atkinson was very pleasant though. The troops weren't impressed at what he'd done to Glass. The US Army has a very strong tradition of not leaving men behind even when they're dead - other, equally professional, armies are often baffled by the risks US troops will take to recover bodies from the battlefield. Much of that tradition comes from the Indian wars, when captured soldiers were often tortured to death. Fitzgerald's attempts to justify his actions just made the situation worse; he claimed that he and Bridger had stayed with Hugh as long as they could, but then been forced to flee when a group of Indians approached. Probably more than a few of his fellow soldiers wondered if he'd be happy to abandon *them*, wounded and helpless, to a raiding party. In any case, their sympathies were with Hugh and they weren't shy about showing it; they had a collection for him and, before he left, presented him with a purse of coins to go with his recovered rifle.

Hugh still felt cheated out of his revenge but he knew the moment had come to choose. He had been the victim of a great wrong, but the perpetrator of it was now protected from him. He could keep obsessing over it, a path that would probably lead to an attempt on Fitzgerald's life and, succeed or fail, retribution from the Army. Alternatively, he could just give thanks that he had his life, and get on with it. It wasn't a hard decision. Standing outside the fort with his familiar rifle in his hands and the purse heavy on his belt, he remembered the face of the cringing, broken man he'd left inside. What had happened a year ago in the upper Missouri Valley was over and done with. Hugh had survived it with his dignity and self-respect intact; John Fitzgerald had not. Hugh hadn't cut him down with a rifle bullet as he'd wanted but he had made sure he could never again hold his head up proudly among the tough, self-sufficient men of the western frontier. Was that enough?

Hugh Glass nodded thoughtfully. Yes, that was enough. As for himself he was alive, and it was time to get on with living. He patted the rifle affectionately, then slung it over his shoulder and set off to the west, back into his beloved mountains.

Chapter 10

By now Hugh was a minor legend in the expanding West. His ordeal with the grizzly was well known, and so were his numerous escapes from the Arikara. He had no trouble finding work in the fur trade or as a scout for the chain of military forts that protected the new territories. Between jobs he hunted on his own, by now as comfortable in the wilderness as the wild animals he stalked. Not long after the final confrontation with Fitzgerald he signed up with a trading party heading for Santa Fe, helping to expand the USA's influence into the southwest. For the next nine years he ranged the length of the western frontier, but he always returned to the region of the Missouri River where his greatest adventures had taken place. It was the place he knew best. Unfortunately it was also where he had enemies. In 1825 he took a Shoshone arrow in the back and had to be evacuated by boat to St. Louis and a surgeon who could extract the barbed head. Over the years that followed he had many more encounters with the Indians, most friendly but a few of them hair-raising. It was inevitable that his luck would run out at last.

As the winter of 1832/33 drew to a close Hugh set out on the first trapping expedition of the new year. It was late March and most of the animals still wore their winter pelts, so he wanted to trap as many as he could before they started to shed the longer, richer hairs. With two companions - Ed Rose and a Frenchman named Menard – he began laying out a trap line along the still-frozen Yellowstone River. Unfortunately, the Arikara were beginning to drift back in from their winter redoubts and raiding parties were prowling the banks. Around the end of the month their paths crossed for the final time.

As the spring thaw gradually set in the snowdrifts were becoming damp and heavy. Plodding through them was hard work. Whenever they could the three Mountain Men stuck to the frozen river, where the wind had swept the open expanse of ice almost clear. It was much easier going and left less of a trail. Unfortunately, it also made them far more visible to watchers on the banks. Their first warning was the ring of hooves on the ice as the attacking warriors accelerated to a gallop.

On foot they had no chance of escaping from the mounted Indians, and the three of them couldn't have held out long. They were all veterans of the frontier, though, and there's no way they would have gone down without a fight. A single volley from their rifles, a couple of pistol shots, then it would have been a desperate flurry of blows delivered with gun butt, ax and knife until the closing ring of assailants finally overwhelmed them. That they were overcome is beyond doubt; Hugh Glass and his two companions were never seen again.

In life Hugh was denied the revenge he sought against his betrayers, but his story wasn't quite finished yet. In April, a group of Indians met a large trapping party led by Johnson Gardner, an old friend of Hugh's. The group claimed they were from the friendly Hidatsa tribe – but then Gardner recognized the rifle one of them was carrying. It was Hugh's. The trappers quickly disarmed and interrogated the Indians, and discovered they were not Hidatsa but Arikaree. That fact, and their possession of the rifle and several other pieces of pilfered equipment, made it clear they were behind the disappearance of the three missing trappers. Enraged, Gardner and his group shot them. Hugh Glass had reached out from beyond the grave through the incriminating evidence of his favorite gun, and a final measure of retribution was served.

Conclusion

Looking back from nearly 200 years further on, it's easy to criticize much of what Hugh Glass and his fellow Mountain Men did. Their expeditions disrupted the traditional way of life of the native people, and had a huge impact on North America's wildlife. At the same time they made the expansion of the USA possible, because without those hardy pioneers there would have been nobody for the settlers of the West to follow.

There's also the cultural impact to consider. Much of the USA's power and wealth today can be traced to the can-do spirit of the people. That spirit was nurtured and grown through the legends of the trailblazers, the scouts and explorers – men like Hugh Glass and his companions. When we talk about the American dream we're harking back to the people whose dreams were big enough and bold enough to carry them beyond the next river or mountain, past the borders of the known world and into new, promising lands. For that alone, never mind the incredible adventures he went through, Hugh Glass deserves his place in history.

[i] The History Herald (April 7, 2013); *Hugh Glass: Mountain Man*
http://www.thehistoryherald.com/Articles/American-History/Civil-War-American-Indian-Wars-Pioneers-1801-1900/hugh-glass-mountain-man
[ii] National Geographic; *Arikara Indians*

http://www.nationalgeographic.com/lewisandclark/record_trib es_020_5_1.html
[iii] PBS; *Lewis and Clark: Arikara Indians*
http://www.pbs.org/lewisandclark/native/ari.html
[iv] HistoryNet (June 12, 2006); *Hugh Glass: Legendary Trapper in America's Western Frontier*
http://www.historynet.com/hugh-glass-legendary-trapper-in-americas-western-frontier.htm
[v] National Geographic; *Casey & Brutus: Grizzly Encounters*
http://natgeotv.com/uk/casey-and-brutus-grizzly-encounters/facts
[vi] HistoryNet (June 12, 2006); *Hugh Glass: Legendary Trapper in America's Western Frontier*
http://www.historynet.com/hugh-glass-legendary-trapper-in-americas-western-frontier.htm
[vii] HistoryNet (June 12, 2006); *Hugh Glass: Legendary Trapper in America's Western Frontier*
http://www.historynet.com/hugh-glass-legendary-trapper-in-americas-western-frontier.htm
[viii] Wandering Lizard California; *Biographical Notes: Hugh Glass*
http://www.inn-california.com/articles/biographic/hughglass1.html

[ix] HistoryNet (June 12, 2006); *Hugh Glass: Legendary Trapper in America's Western Frontier*

http://www.historynet.com/hugh-glass-legendary-trapper-in-americas-western-frontier.htm

[x] Wandering Lizard California; *Biographical Notes: Hugh Glass*
http://www.inn-california.com/articles/biographic/hughglass1.html

[xi] Wandering Lizard California; *Biographical Notes: Hugh Glass*
http://www.inn-california.com/articles/biographic/hughglass1.html

CPSIA information can be obtained at www.ICGtesting.com
Printed in the USA
LVOW07s1333130116

470469LV00025B/852/P